An Introduction to Coping with

Post-Traumatic Stress

An Introduction to Coping with
Post-Traumatic Stress
2nd Edition

Ann Wetmore

ROBINSON

ROBINSON

First published in Great Britain in 2019 by Robinson

1 3 5 7 9 10 8 6 4 2

Author's Note
Sincere thanks to N.S. designer Bruce Trick for his depiction of
PTSD symptom clusters in the Glasses of Water illustration

Important note
This book is not intended as a substitute for medical advice or
treatment. Any person with a condition requiring medical attention
should consult a qualified medical practitioner or suitable therapist.

A CIP catalogue record for this book
is available from the British Library.

ISBN: 978-1-47214-016-6

Typeset in Bembo by Initial Typesetting Services, Edinburgh
Printed and bound in Great Britain by Clays Ltd, Elcograf S.p.A.

Papers used by Robinson are from well-managed forests and
other responsible sources.

MIX
Paper from
responsible sources
FSC
www.fsc.org FSC® C104740

Robinson
An imprint of
Little, Brown Book Group
Carmelite House
50 Victoria Embankment
London EC4Y 0DZ

An Hachette UK Company
www.hachette.co.uk
www.littlebrown.co.uk

Contents

About This Book

Traumatic events are so extremely stressful that most people find themselves completely overwhelmed for a short while, and often for some time afterwards. In the space of a few seconds, the impact of a catastrophic experience can turn lives upside-down, and leave people disoriented, anxious, and in a state of disbelief about what has just happened.

Situations such as car crashes, robberies, job loss after years of loyal employment, or sudden death of a loved one can be very difficult to cope with, and may leave us numb or angry and closed off for days or weeks until life settles down again.

If you've gone through a terrible experience and found that the intense reactions that you had from it refuse to go away or that pieces of the memory continue to interfere with your life, this book may be helpful to you. The material presented is meant to serve as a starting point, to help you understand your reactions and to put in place some new coping strategies. It's likely to be most useful for people whose lingering post-traumatic reactions came from a single event where they experienced horror, loss or injury. Those who have unfortunately been caught up in long-term traumatic situations, such as domestic violence, physical and sexual abuse, hostage-takings, or combat situations may find this material a useful beginning, but are likely to need additional professional help to deal with their complex post-trauma feelings and reactions.

If you (or someone you know) have been suffering with issues of post-traumatic stress, Part 1 of this book will help you gain a clearer understanding of your reactions and why they are not going away. Part 2 contains practical strategies for you to work through by reading, writing and reflecting on your thoughts and behaviours. This material was designed for you to work through on your own, but if, at any point, it feels like too much for you to continue with alone, please talk to your doctor about additional resources, which may include help from a qualified therapist, or medication.

While it's natural to wish for an instant answer or a 'magic' solution, many post-traumatic conditions are so complicated that healing becomes a lengthy and uneven process, with gains and set-backs to be expected. Go slowly but keep working at it!

May all your efforts lead to healing after your trauma.

Ann Wetmore

A Cautious Reminder

This book is intended as a self-help guide and as a first step in managing post-traumatic stress symptoms. It's *not* an instant answer, nor is it a speedy solution for PTS reactions. While a range of treatment options are suggested, it does *not* represent all treatment possibilities, and the book is not meant to be a substitute for ongoing therapy with a trained professional.

It's hoped that this book will be a practical, readily available resource to get you started on a recovery route, and to help you to understand better what has been contributing to your distress after trauma. It may also be useful while you're waiting for a referral to a treatment programme, or as a home-based workbook to supplement sessions with a practitioner in cognitive behavioural therapy.

Like all healthcare interventions, the intention behind this material is to **do no harm**. If the CBT approach, on which this book is based, does not feel like the right 'match' for you, or, **if you feel your symptoms are in any way worsening** while you're using this material, and leading you to consider self-harm or high-risk actions, **please speak openly about this to your doctor** and explore other options through the healthcare system.

Part 1: ABOUT POST-TRAUMATIC STRESS

1

What *Is* Post-Traumatic Stress?

'Trauma' comes from the Greek word meaning 'wound'. While emotional wounds are usually internal and invisible, post-traumatic stress reactions, like flashbacks, high arousal, crippling self-blame, extreme avoidance/withdrawal, etc. are the noticeable signs of emotional injury that do not stay under the surface.

When we are called upon to perform under difficult circumstances, meet challenges and deal with disappointments and crises, we may feel alarmed, but usually we can muster up our coping resources, tough it out, and get through. The difference with a traumatic event is that the experience is so extraordinarily stressful that it goes beyond anything we ever expected to happen, or anything we could have thought of as 'normal' and been prepared to handle.

Because traumatic events are both terrible and terrifying, if you have had such an experience – like being a passenger in an awful car crash, receiving a violent assault or witnessing a severe workplace injury/death – you probably felt overwhelmed and horrified. Your body may have gone into shock, combined with surges of adrenaline, and you may have acted as if you were stuck on 'auto-pilot'. For days or even weeks after the incident, you may have had difficulty concentrating, been unable to sleep for any length of time, and perhaps you found yourself replaying the incident over and over in your mind, or having nightmares about it. You may have continued to feel numb, like you're 'going through the motions' but not really 'there', and you may have tried *not* to think about it or found yourself obsessively thinking about it all the time. Perhaps you blamed yourself for part of it, thinking, '***I should have seen it coming!***' All of these descriptions are very typical post-traumatic stress responses. Usually, after some time has passed, the reactions gradually subside – the incident is not forgotten, but ceases to interfere, for the most part, with everyday life – but not always.

Why can't I get past this? These reactions keep coming back!!

It is the overwhelming nature of the traumatic experience that often causes a sense of personal violation and makes it difficult to resolve. Despite coping ability and perceived resilience, no one is truly immune. The internalised *meaning* of the event may change your view of yourself. For example:

'Eddie' pictured himself as a really good coper, able to tackle almost anything, all the while taking care of others. One morning, while he was standing on a street corner with his children, waiting for the crossing signal, a large delivery vehicle came hurtling around the corner, out of control due to failed brakes, and headed straight for them. Faced with this sudden crisis situation, Eddie *froze*, and could not move, although his children spontaneously dived out of the way. Fortunately, the driver was able to stop at the very last minute, and no one was physically hurt.

Later, because he had not been able to act quickly to protect his children, Eddie was filled with a deep sense of *shame and self-loathing*. His internal view of himself was profoundly altered. He had lost his sense of belief in himself as a strong person who could be relied upon to protect his family.

Although Eddie's children had also gone through this near-miss incident and had been very frightened at the time, a few days later they were back to feeling like themselves and going on with their normal activities. They expressed surprise when Eddie mentioned that he was still thinking about what '*might* have happened' and stressing that they needed to be extra-careful about crossing the street. They even teased him a little bit, saying, '*Oh dad, now you think there's danger at every corner!*' Of course, their safety was exactly what Eddie was obsessively worried about, and he felt even more shame that his family was getting on with their lives and he was ineffective at being able to help them.

How do I know if I have PTSD?

Post-Traumatic Stress Disorder (PTSD) is the only clinical condition that is diagnosed as the result of what has happened *to* you, events that you **experienced** or were directly **exposed to** that were so catastrophic that 'life changed in a heartbeat', as some survivors have said. During a real or perceived threat to your survival or personal safety, such as witnessing extreme violence or being caught up in a mass evacuation or terror incident, the way you understand natural justice and predict your own behaviour and that of others may be drastically altered.

People will usually recount such experiences with statements such as: *'I really thought I was going to die'* . . . *'I didn't think we would make it through'* . . . *'I thought I was a goner'* . . . *'I could not believe what I was seeing in front of me – it was so horrible, and I couldn't stop it!'* . . . *'I thought I would split apart!'*

Individuals such as first responders, emergency health workers, fire, police, military, etc., are trained for and expected to deal with situations involving danger, violence, severe injuries and the witnessing of death. For these people, repeated exposure often has a cumulative impact, but post-traumatic reactions may not emerge until much later. Delayed PTSD may eventually be triggered by a particularly gruesome case or an extraordinarily stressful aspect of something going on in their present lives, on top of years of accumulated traumatic stress.

Do my symptoms fit a PTSD pattern?

Post-Traumatic Stress Disorder has long been defined by core clusters of Intrusion, Avoidance and Arousal symptoms. Recently, the medical, psychiatric and psychological professions have updated their diagnostic criteria (DSM-5, 2013) by the addition of a fourth category, Persistent Negative Thought/Mood.

In order to fit the newer definition of PTSD, these disturbing reactions must occur as a result of a traumatic exposure, such as threatened death, violent assault, serious injury, sexual violation, witnessing severe harm to loved ones, or through occupational or combat handling of violence and death. The symptoms in these four psychological distress areas (whether they arise immediately or are delayed and occur later) must continue beyond one month.

Glasses of water

The PTSD symptom pattern can be depicted as four cylindrical glass containers on a tray. The amount of 'liquid' contained in each glass may fluctuate, as symptoms

*are triggered and then remit, but the containers remain
stable on the tray (which represents exposure) and continue
for one month.*

Each category involves a cluster of emotional reactions which may vary in intensity and fluctuate
in how frequently they intrude from day to day.
Whether the onset of symptoms has been immediate
or delayed, they must have been present for at least
one month and be continuing for the condition to
be considered PTSD.

Symptoms of post-traumatic stress disorder in detail (do any apply to you?)

This could be used as your checklist:

INTRUSION

❑ **Flashbacks** – you feel like the trauma is lit-
erally **happening all over again**, often with
vivid sensory experiences of sound, smell,
sight, etc.

❑ **Intrusive memories** – you get vivid recollections of 'pieces' of the traumatic event; you
can't stop thinking about certain aspects of the
experience; horror images keep popping into
mind as if your brain is stuck there.

❑ You might also be unable to recall other important details – your memory has 'missing pieces'.

❑ **Upsetting dreams/nightmares** – your dreams may be like re-living the experience in sleep and may connect to the **arousal cluster** of symptoms, as you wake sweating and terrified; your nightmares may be **worse** than what actually happened, as they may symbolise your worst fears or represent the deepest terror connected to how you felt during the event.

❑ **Memory 'triggers'** – a small occurrence in everyday life, such as a sound, smell, a look on someone's face or a news broadcast, may set off a chain of memory 'bits' and you have intense distress reactions associated with them.

❑ **Feeling 'triggers'** – sometimes referred to as 'feeling flashbacks', where being in an anxious/aroused state that resembles feelings experienced during the traumatic event (for example, being squeezed and jostled by the crowd while waiting to get on a train) will trigger reactions such as profound fear, twitching or a sense of utter helplessness that's an over-the-top response to the current situation.

AVOIDANCE

❑ You make serious **efforts to avoid** any thoughts, feelings, persons, activities or locations that could remind you of the trauma, even those very remotely linked to the event.

❑ You **change your behaviou**r so that memories of the trauma won't be triggered.

❑ You **pull away from others** so that you won't have to explain your reactions: 'I don't have the words to tell you what happened to me.'

❑ You **avoid social activitie**s or celebrations, especially if you would be expected to take a lead role or even make general conversation about how things are going for you: 'I'm not the person I was before.'

❑ You **put off** even short-term **future plans**.

PERSISTENT NEGATIVE THOUGHT/
MOOD

❑ You have new and/or **exaggerated negative beliefs** about yourself.

❑ You **blame yourself** for aspects of the trauma that you could not possibly have foreseen.

❑ You feel ultra-responsible, or **permanently harmed or changed**.

❑ You **doubt your ability** to cope with even simple things that would not have been a problem before.

❑ You feel **isolated and set apart** from others.

❑ You **cannot remember important aspects** of the trauma(s) and feel that is your fault.

❑ You feel **emotionally numb**, and have persistent **difficulty experiencing positive emotions** like satisfaction, happiness or loving feelings, in a way that you didn't before.

❑ You feel **set apart and detached** from activities or causes that used to be important to you.

❑ You **dwell on negative aspects** of the world and yourself in an exaggerated way, such as: '*The world is dangerous*', '*No one can be trusted*', '*I'm not safe to be around*'.

❑ You feel **'doomed' or 'jinxed'**.

AROUSAL

❑ You feel **keyed-up or 'hyper'** all the time.

❑ You're uncharacteristically **irritable**; you have angry **outbursts** or outraged confrontations with others, which is not like your normal self.

❑ You're constantly **scanning for danger** and

you have **extreme startle reaction**s when surprised by something trivial.

❑ You **can't fall asleep** – you're **'afraid' to sleep**, and you have difficulty staying asleep or going back to sleep when wakened.

❑ You have **problems** (not present before the trauma) **maintaining concentration** or focus on tasks.

❑ You've become **hyper-sensitive to loud/ sudden noises.**

❑ You engage in **reckless** or potentially **self-harming behaviours** or significantly increase **substance abuse**.

I have *some* of those symptoms but *not all of them* – does this mean that I don't really have PTSD?

You don't need all of the symptoms in each category to be diagnosed as having PTSD. Each category involves a cluster of emotional reactions which may vary in intensity and fluctuate in how frequently they are present from day to day. *Sometimes one symptom cluster will be much more active,* for example, feeling on 'red alert' all day, even without flashbacks or avoidance, or having many flashbacks and 'mini-memory-flashes' even when you're consciously not avoiding any part of your normal activities. Whether the onset of symptoms has been immediate or delayed, they must have been present for at least one **month** and be continuing for the condition to be considered PTSD.

For some, not getting a full diagnosis of PTSD will affect whether they receive legal compensation or qualify for disability or injury claims. Obviously, diagnosis requires a full assessment from several qualified practitioners, and you shouldn't make assumptions on your own from the list on the previous pages.

Why is this bothering me now? I thought I had dealt with it years ago?

For some people, post-traumatic stress symptoms emerge long after a major event, sometimes as a result of a current, fairly minor stressor that triggers a whole series of suppressed reactions. This is what happened to Helen:

HELEN'S STORY

'I had been involved for a long time with a man who was very abusive to me, physically and emotionally. After I separated from him, it took several years of counselling at the Women's Centre in my community for me to really feel I was in control of my life and that I had come to terms with understanding and getting past the post-traumatic stress reactions that had been with me for so long. Then, recently, out of the blue, while I was running on the treadmill at the gym, a man bumped into me from behind by accident, and I fell on the still-moving treadmill and was horribly scraped and bleeding. I came down so hard, I thought my elbow was broken. The two staff on duty at the gym that evening were both young and had only been working there a few weeks – once they saw me stand up and move, they didn't even contact the manager. I had to drive myself, in a dazed condition, to the hospital, where I waited for several hours in the emergency unit before I was seen.

Although it turned out that my elbow was only badly bruised, and my scraped skin did heal, in the weeks that followed, many of my PTSD symptoms returned: I was jumpy, nothing felt safe, and I was very emotional and hyper-reactive to anything that startled me. I had a lot of trouble sleeping, with some nightmares of being attacked. The worst trigger was that I had felt physically hurt and completely helpless, and no one took me seriously at the time. I started to doubt myself again and wondered if I would ever get over this or if I was someone who made too much fuss, who couldn't cope with little bumps from life!'

Regardless of whether you have all the signs, or whether *some* symptoms and behaviours that you didn't have before your trauma are now having a terrible impact on your life, it's important that, rather than waiting and hoping for these feelings just to go away, you look for effective ways to manage what is going on and begin to claim your life back. This book is unlikely to be the final solution, but it may serve as a **powerful first step** in leading you to **recognise your needs and determine your future steps** better, as well as helping you to **communicate better with your doctor and others** about your condition.

Part 2: COPING WITH POST-TRAUMATIC STRESS REACTIONS

2

Your Self-Directed Cognitive Behavioural Therapy Programme

'What can I do about all these PTS reactions? I don't think I'll ever get over this! I just want to feel "normal" again!'

The self-directed programme presented in this book is based on **Cognitive Behavioural Therapy**, a widely researched and empirically validated psychological treatment system that has been effective in improving coping patterns for people across a wide variety of situations (Beck, Aaron T. et al., 1987).

What is Cognitive Behavioural Therapy? How does it work?

CBT, as it's known in shortened form, focuses on identifying and changing your thought patterns, because it's believed that your thoughts, and how you interpret situations, influence your emotional reactions and that your behaviour follows from this.

It works like this: if your perception of a situation is distorted and produces exaggerated negative thoughts (*'I dropped mustard on my shirt at lunch, now everyone is looking at me and laughing while I'm waiting in this queue . . . I'm so clumsy!'*), the feelings that arise almost simultaneously are uncomfortable and negative, and may result in you leaving the situation early and perhaps avoiding similar situations in the future, or obsessively thinking about it afterwards.

Core beliefs about yourself and the world are likely to be at the heart of your interpretations, and may contribute to catastrophising, thinking in 'black and white', or 'all or nothing' terms, perfectionism, procrastination, or dismissing positive aspects of your behaviour or achievements. These are common thinking patterns that most of us experience at some point, but when they are too often present, they can be debilitating.

Using CBT techniques, if you're able to *recognise* negative patterns and *change* what you're thinking, different feelings and behaviours are likely to follow. (*'Sometimes I jump to the worst conclusion, especially when I get anxious . . . those people might have been sharing a joke amongst themselves . . . it was only a small splodge of mustard anyway . . . my thinking goes over-the-top when I get worried . . . I'll eat more carefully next time.'*)

Links in the chain of automatic thoughts and reactions

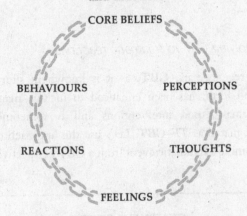

CORE BELIEFS

BEHAVIOURS   PERCEPTIONS

REACTIONS   THOUGHTS

FEELINGS

Recognise the links in the chain: core beliefs –
influence perceptions – influence thoughts – influence
feelings – influence reactions and behaviours.

What can this CBT programme do for me?

Even though your thoughts, feelings and reactions
are linked together at lightning speed, identifying
the core beliefs that influence this chain and recognising how your traumatic experiences are likely to
impact your perception of a situation, can support
your efforts to understand your reactions and give
you more choices about how to respond, instead of
reacting automatically. This may help you build a

sense of 'new normal' instead of being stuck at the time of your trauma.

Applying CBT to traumatic reactions

In recent years, **CBT**, as it is known in short-ened form, has been enhanced to include many trauma-focused interventions and is sometimes designated as **TF-CBT**. Let's use this approach to examine a traumatic event from a CBT perspective:

CYNTHIA'S STORY

Cynthia, age seventeen, had her first summer job working at a fast-food restaurant. She was cycling to work a morning shift when a car hit her, and she found herself hurtling through the air and hitting the pavement with her body sideways. She suffered a broken arm, multiple scrapes and bruises, and a severely swollen face.

Although both the ambulance attendants and, later, the hospital workers, assured her that her injuries would heal, and that there would be no permanent damage, she was convinced that she would never be the

---

same again. Over and over she had memory flashes of seeing the gravel and dirt of the road coming up to hit her face, and she was afraid even to look at her mangled bicycle. For months, she had nightmares about being attacked and harmed.

Because Cynthia had so much trouble getting to sleep, and staying asleep, due to violent and disturbing dreams, she started taking several (alcoholic) drinks before bedtime as a way to 'wind down'. The amount she drank increased as time went on.

Cynthia's persistent thoughts:

'I'm not safe when I'm biking. I'm really unlucky. I'm ashamed of being so frightened. I can't sleep. My face looks awful and everyone is noticing. I wish I had never taken that job! I'll never get over this. My friend Jane had a bike crash a few months ago and she handled it really well – what's wrong with me?'

Cynthia's resulting behaviours:

She became too anxious to bike to work, so she spent almost all her wages on cabs if she was unable to get a ride with co-workers. She requested work shifts where she would

> be out back doing food preparation, in order
> to avoid serving people at the front counter,
> as she was sure her scarred face would put
> them off their food. She constantly com-
> pared herself to her friend Jane, and others,
> who had recovered quickly from cycling
> crashes, and labelled herself as 'jinxed', and
> 'a loser who can't cope like other people'.

In reading over Cynthia's reactions and behaviours after her accident, you probably realised how
extreme her thoughts and feelings had become, and
that her exaggerated interpretations would leave
her stuck at the time of her trauma. She is now
hyper-alert to danger, avoids biking, makes negative comparisons of herself to others, predicts future
distress, has sleep problems and growing alcohol
issues, continues to catastrophise, etc.

By referring back to the 'Glasses of Water' PTSD
symptom illustration on page 8, you can see that
Cynthia's reactions do reflect the four symptom
clusters of PTSD. She has: **Intrusive** recollections,
Avoidance behaviours, high **Arousal** related to
her traumatic injury, and exaggerated and persistent
Negative Beliefs about herself.

What to do?

The CBT process requires attention, focus, 'fierce' commitment on your part and some recording work with pencil and paper (or e-devices) in order to raise your awareness of those rapid, almost-automatic thoughts that trigger debilitating emotions. The important thing to remember is that it can work for you if you give it a serious try.

How to talk yourself out of trying this CBT programme

> *'I find it hard to accept that my thoughts influence how I feel and that if I can change my thoughts, I might react to things differently.'*

It's not necessary to be positive, but to remain open and flexible in your thinking. Chapter 3 of this book will help you to put this CBT method into action.

3

Starting Your Self-Treatment Cognitive Behavioural Programme

You'll need:

* a notebook (or electronic device) to write in

* safe surroundings to work in

* safe time limits

Your notebook (or e-device)

The paper version can be of any size or shape, lined or unlined, and sufficiently robust to last through a number of weeks of daily entries. You'll be doing a lot of *self-monitoring*; by that we mean keeping track of your thoughts, feelings and behaviours, recording them in your notebook of choice, and re-reading what you have written in order to reflect on it, recognise patterns, and to make small goals that you can target for change. Because this is a very personal recording activity, you will need to safeguard the privacy of your notes, and ensure that this material is not being read by others without your permission. If you are keeping your notes by electronic means, such as on your phone, laptop, or other computer, create a special password-protected file, or delete material on other devices once you have transferred it for safe storage. If you choose the traditional paper notebook or diary for your entries, locate a secure place – that could be a locked drawer, a suitcase or a filing cabinet with a lock, or even an inexpensive toolbox from a building supply store that has a locking capacity. Respect your own right to privacy, and make it easy for others to do so by not leaving your personal writing out in the open and available to curious eyes.

Safe surroundings

It is important that you have some privacy when you are working on these recovery tasks. It can be difficult to find many uninterrupted moments if you are living in the midst of a busy family, or if your living situation is crowded and chaotic. Do what you can to reduce stress in your living circumstances, and to find a spot where you can make your notes unobserved, even if that means that you need to work in short bursts and reflect later on what you've written. If you are finding things chaotic, it may be tempting to consider a drastic change such as moving, selling your home or leaving your job. However, unless there are dramatic reasons behind these considerations (such as dangerous surroundings, threat of bankruptcy, or violence in the home), it's usually best to **postpone major decisions if possible**, while you concentrate on finding relief for some of your post-traumatic distress. If you're in doubt, consult a trusted professional (maybe start with your family doctor) and don't be hasty about your decisions, as the PTS symptoms tend to 'move' with you, if unresolved.

Safe time limits

Set yourself **time limits** for your self-monitoring notes, and stop immediately if you become unduly upset. Ten or twenty minutes at one go might be enough, or you may be able to work for as long as an hour sometimes. It will likely vary from day to day, but it's recommended that you don't exceed an hour at a sitting. This is a process that's intended to *do no harm* to yourself or to others, so you must take careful responsibility not to do too much at one time and to keep yourself safe while you are dealing with volatile feelings. It's **best not to do your writing work really late at night**, as you're likely to reduce your chances for a sound sleep when you're emotionally wound up.

Getting started: Ways you might talk yourself out of starting the CBT self-treatment programme

I don't like writing things down.

I don't like thinking about it.

I just want these feelings to go away.

I don't believe that changing my thoughts or the way I look at things will make a difference.

This feels like too much work.

Of course, your thoughts may be full of doubts and hesitations, like the statements above. You can stop the programme at any time and take it up later if you choose. It's all under your control. You've already gone through very difficult times and survived. Let's continue for now . . .

Self-assessment: How are you coping now?

Think over these questions thoroughly and write your answers in your notebook of choice.

- How has your coping behaviour changed since your traumatic event?

- Do you sleep? How well? Do you have night-mares or vivid night-time recollections?

- Has your temper changed? Are you getting into arguments with others, or even anticipating an argument?

- Do you drink more than you did before? How much more?

- If you've been prescribed medications, are you taking these properly?

- Can you finish tasks?

- Do you find it unusually hard to be intimate and loving? Are you avoiding friends?

- Are you living in the past, and re-living the trauma? Are memories haunting you?

- Are there certain things about that traumatic experience that you're keeping to yourself that you've never told anyone?

- Are you 'fibbing' to your doctor about how well you are, or leaving out important health details or symptoms that you're worried about?

- Are you 'fibbing' to yourself? Are you living in fear?

Recording phase

You do not need to answer all of the above questions in one sitting. There may be some that take more pondering, and you **may need to come back to this 'coping self-assessment' at times and adjust your answers**, or even **record how you might have improved (or worsened) over time**. Be honest! Because different areas are targeted, some may get better with attention, and some may go in the opposite direction. The goal here is to help you pinpoint your specific problem areas and assist you in developing improved ways to manage them.

You may recognise that some of your problem areas correspond to the PTSD symptom clusters shown in the Glasses of Water illustration (page 8), and, it may help you to get a clearer picture by grouping your answers into those four categories.

Coping strategy: Managing your breathing

While working on your trauma notes (and under other stressful circumstances), you may have noticed yourself getting anxious, and your breathing rate changing – sometimes getting rapid and shallow. Runners, athletes, those who practise yoga, speech makers, exam-takers, etc. will all confirm that they had to learn to pay attention to their breathing rate, and sometimes change the style and depth of their breathing to perform more effectively. We're going to use this same principle to teach you to 'tune into' your breathing and practise using it as a calming, stress-reducing technique. Although it's not a solution in itself, *managed breathing is a very valuable tool in your personal CBT programme and available to you at any time.*

At times, especially as a young person, when you became over-anxious or over-excited, you might have been told, 'Just take a deep breath', or, 'Take a few deep breaths'. That was probably easier said than done! When you're anxious, your chest muscles tend to tighten up and your breathing becomes shallow. Air only reaches the top part of your lungs! When you're trying to gulp in more air, it feels impossible, and may result in short, rapid breaths that raise your anxiety level, rather than lowering it. There's a more effective way to control your breathing and achieve the desired result, a slower, deeper breath – it's called the **'Count to Calm Breathing Method'** (see the box opposite):

The Count to Calm Breathing Method:

1. *EXHALE FIRST.* Purse your lips and blow out through your mouth, like you're blowing through a wide drinking straw. Push out as much air as possible.

2. *INHALE* through your nose to the count of four: 1 - 2 - 3 - 4.

3. *HOLD* that breath to the count of five: 1 - 2 - 3 - 4 - 5.

4. *BREATHE OUT* through your mouth, exhaling fully, to the count of six, releasing that last bit of air out at the end: 1 - 2 - 3 - 4 - 5 - 6.

5. *BREATHE IN* through your nose again, letting your body automatically take this breath in more deeply to the count of four: 1 - 2 - 3 - 4. HOLD to the count of 5, then BREATHE OUT through your mouth to the count of 6.

6. *CONTINUE* until you have finished THREE COMPLETE BREATHS.

With each complete breath, you will notice that the air is reaching more deeply into your lungs, and feels like it is going further down into your belly. Your breathing rate by the end is probably slower, and your heart rate has likely stopped racing. Use the Count to Calm Breathing Method whenever you notice that you are getting tense or anxious, or struggling to manage your feelings in difficult situations. Just three complete breaths with this method are enough to help you clear your head and gain a bit more control over your reactions in the moment. (This is a self-management technique, *not* an avoidance strategy. It does not mean that your issues are resolved, or that you don't have to face what is upsetting you, just that you can be less overwhelmed by anxious thoughts and able to think more clearly.)

Reflection phase

- Look over what you've written in your notebook. Pick out one or two areas that you would rate as the worst; that is, *what's troubling you the most*? Is it: flashbacks, or memories that intrude while you're awake and trying to get on with things? Can't sleep or having nightmares?

- If you say, *'I just can't cope!'*, that statement is too vague – you need to be more specific. What is it that you can't cope with? When are you most overwhelmed? Are you hypersensitive to noise or over-reacting to every little thing that startles you? Are you angry all the time?

- Designate a reaction area to target and form a simple goal, for example: *'I will keep track on a calendar or in my notebook of how often I have flashbacks, and rate them from 1 to 10 about how severe and debilitating they are.'* Note the time of day that they occur and identify any triggers that might have set them off. The table below is a good example of how to do this.

Situation	How I reacted	How intense	How I felt afterwards
Fireworks outside at New Year's Party	Flashback to explosion/ trauma	8 out of 10	Embarrassed – I dived under the dining table!

Coping with flashbacks and intrusive memories

Whether they occur during daytime or in the middle of a dream, flashbacks feel like you're re-living the trauma all over again. Sights, sounds, smells, the sense of things rubbing against your skin, all seem to be happening *now*, in the present time. Intrusive memories are like pieces of your traumatic experience that repeat and repeat and repeat. You're aware that they are remembered fragments, but, because they're such disturbing memories, they *intrude upon*, or take over, your thinking when they occur. Both flashbacks and intrusive memories can last for different lengths of time (even a few seconds or a few minutes can be very disturbing) and the memories, especially, often differ in how intense and upsetting they are. It may feel like your mind is stuck on replay of certain scenes and that you're powerless in your struggle to get past these pieces of automatic recall.

Why do they happen?

Flashbacks seem to come out of the blue and take over, so that you feel you're out of control, or even losing your mind. There are some theories that describe flashbacks as your brain continuing to try to make sense of a traumatic experience that was so overwhelming when it happened that there was no frame of reference for your mind to be able to file it away or relate it to anything you knew or expected before. Thus, the raw experience keeps repeating over and over in your brain: images, smells, sounds and feelings from the traumatic incident that violated your assumptions about life and natural justice. Although right now you might feel at the mercy of the memories popping into your mind, it's not hopeless! Beginning to pay attention, tracking any patterns, understanding how intrusions are set off and recognising any triggers can help you to re-establish even a tiny bit of your sense of control.

Triggers

Here are two real-life accounts from individuals who had struggled to cope with flashbacks and intrusive memories. Following highly traumatic experiences, both Paul and Carla (not their real names) had been in treatment for PTSD for some months with a cognitive behavioural therapist and later described what had been most helpful in getting them to recognise triggers and move towards recovery.

PAUL'S STORY

'I had a lot of flashbacks and intrusive thoughts and terrible images (some worse than the actual trauma) that kept coming into my mind. Once I accepted that these were not necessarily *true* or *accurate*, but were actually symptoms of PTSD, my thoughts changed. Instead of thinking, *"I'll never get over this"*, I started to think, *"This is normal for me, right now."* *"There's nothing wrong with me...this is a symptom, and I have to pay attention to what triggered it."* I no longer got into that cycle of worry and fretting about the flashbacks and images. When I started to think about them as symptoms, it became more about what I was doing to set them off, like when I aggravate my bad back and I have to figure out what triggered that back pain.'

CARLA'S STORY

'I came to regard my flashbacks and intrusive memories like "unfinished business" that my brain was trying to get me to understand. What was most helpful to me was to repeat to myself over and over, "*This is a memory – it's not happening now!*" I tried to ground myself in the present and pay more attention to sights and sounds around me that helped me focus on the here and now. I also deliberately *reduced my exposure* to potential "triggers" by not going to movies or watching TV programmes that I anticipated would have distressing scenes, even if they were only remotely related to the trauma I had gone through (such as watching violent situations with people being helpless). I kept my surroundings as calm as possible and watched very few news reports for quite a long time.'

4

Tackling Disturbed Sleep

Almost all the people who describe the after-effects of traumatic experiences report that their sleep was disrupted for some time after the incident. Many survivors are afraid to go to sleep, because they find themselves re-living their traumas through horrific, vivid dreams or through nightmares. If you are having sleep terrors like this, the content could be different from what actually happened to you, but the bad dreams might touch indirectly on your deepest fears (such as '*I dreamt I was about to be killed by a hooded assassin*'), and the terror you lived through. If your sleep has been disrupted for weeks or months, it has likely had devastating effects on your own functioning, and your intimate relationships have likely suffered as well. If you're waking drenched in cold sweat, and your sleeping partner says you've been thrashing and calling out through the night, you're left feeling embarrassed and responsible for unconscious reactions that are impossible to control, and the bedroom may feel like an unsafe place for you both.

It's very tempting to turn to alcohol, hoping it will help you to suppress your feelings and recollections and also serve as a 'sleep aid'! Unfortunately, over-drinking is not an effective form of sleep medication – it tends to add one problem on to another. You may fall asleep, but you're likely to wake in a few hours anxious and disoriented, and if you get back to sleep later, you'll still be having bad dreams. The after-effects of the alcohol contribute to depressed feelings and the temptation to drink more to block those out may be strong.

If you're trying to cope with disturbed sleep that's part of your post-traumatic stress reactions, it's vital that you scale back your drinking or give up altogether for a period of time. If that seems impossible, consider visiting one of the many organisations (such as Alcoholics Anonymous) that offer valuable support for reducing or stopping drinking. As the name indicates, Alcoholics Anonymous groups keep your identity anonymous and have helpful literature available, both in print and online.

Sleep medications may be an occasional or short-term solution but should only be prescribed and monitored by your doctor. Refuse recreational drugs and be cautious about the use of over-the-counter products that claim to regulate sleep. Often, they are not very effective for people whose sleep problems originate with post-traumatic stress, and it's tempting to overuse them, rather than to tell your family doctor about underlying issues and discuss effective alternatives. Never take anyone else's prescription, whether for sleep disturbance or anything else.

Keeping a sleep diary

Your notebook can serve as a 'sleep calendar', or 'sleep diary', in which you record the patterns of your sleep, a week at a time. Draw seven blocks, one for each day of the week (or insert a pre-prepared calendar page), and use these to write:

- a number rating (0 to 10) for the quality of your sleep the night before ('I would rate that a 3 out of 10')

- an estimate of how many hours sleep you did get, even if the sleep was broken ('about 3½ hours altogether')

- how you felt when waking in the morning ('exhausted', 'discouraged')

- any occurrence that you can identify, however small, that may have contributed to a terrible dream later or served as a trigger for a sleeping flashback

Opposite is an example of how your Sleep Diary might look.

Day:	MON.	TUES.	WED.	THURS.	FRI.	SAT.	SUN.
Rating:	3/10	4/10	4/10	2/10	4.5/10	2/10	4.5/10
Hours of sleep:	3.5	4	4.5	3	5	2.5	4.5
I felt:	upset	exhausted	terrified	hopeless	numb	agitated	confused

Things that happened:

Monday, I ran into a former co-worker and tried to avoid conversation.

Wednesday, I was walking by a shop and I saw a jersey in the window like the one I was wearing on the day the trauma happened. I felt really upset.

Friday, loud noises at the pub got me really shaking.

Changing your 'sleep attitude'

Yes, you're being asked to take on the role of becoming your own 'sleep detective'! As you've probably already realised, when you're sleep-deprived it has a devastating effect on your mood state and your ability to concentrate effectively. It's very easy to slip into negative thinking, especially in that 'all or nothing' pattern mentioned earlier.

> *'I'll never get over this!'* . . . *'It's hopeless.'.* . . .
> *'I can't go on like this.'* . . . *'I'll be messed-up
> like this forever!'* . . . *'I'm no good to anyone.'*

Saying or thinking things like this to yourself can promote destructive impulses and risky behaviour, such as reckless driving, tempting fate by walking alone at night in unsafe areas, careless crossing of the street in heavy traffic or depriving yourself of food as a way of punishing yourself. Take yourself out of harm's way by committing to suspend those 'always-or-never' habits of thinking and begin to 'observe' on paper (or electronically) what's really going on with your sleep.

Becoming a bit more objective and keeping notes about your sleep patterns provides clues to help you form an improved coping plan. Rather than merely saying that you'll continue to carry on, and tough it out, the same way you've been doing, you may now be able to recognise factors that have contributed to poor sleep during the week that has just gone by.

There may have been extra stress at work, project deadlines or arguments at home, or perhaps you've been deliberately staying too busy to think about anything, worrying right up until the time that you go to bed, so then thoughts you've been pushing away come out during sleep when your guard is down.

As you reflect on your sleep notes, you might also recognise reminders that occurred out of the blue and triggered bad dreams later, such as a flash of something that you saw out of the corner of your eye, a remembered smell or sound or being involved in an embarrassing incident.

Identifying such triggers can be a valuable step in understanding why your sleep was so poor at a particular time. You have more *clues* to help you put the pieces together, and you won't feel so helpless.

As your sleep attitude begins to shift slightly to the positive, try out new 'coping statements' that could help you feel a bit more in control. These might sound like: *'This is temporary'* . . . *'I am trying out new ways to cope'* . . . *'There are steps I can take to help myself to improve my sleep'*. Try to generate some in your own words and record them.

_____

_____

_____

_____

_____

_____

Practical coping arrangements for sleep

*   Remember to use your managed breathing skill! The **Count to Calm** breathing method (page 33) is available for your use anytime and may be especially helpful as you try to settle down to sleep.

- Slowly counting as you breathe in through your nose, hold, and breathe out completely through your mouth helps you to settle and turn off some of your 'worry thoughts' about how you'll sleep tonight. If you do wake in a startled, hyper-aroused state, use the *Count to Calm* method to help you reorientate to a waking state and bring your breathing down to a more normal rate.

- Remember to blow out forcefully first to begin the breathing rhythm.

- If you have a bed partner who has been very disturbed by your PTS reactions during sleep, you may need to make a temporary arrangement to sleep elsewhere in your home, or to move to a different bed or the sofa if you're having a bad time on a particular night. It's useful to explain why you're doing this beforehand (for example, say that you're trying to master new ways of coping with your disturbed sleep and you want to minimise disruption to your partner), so that the other person doesn't feel shut out or rejected when you switch to another spot.

- Avoid caffeinated drinks before bedtime, or even from late afternoon onwards, and try as much as possible to establish a routine that helps you relax a bit: this might include listening to soft music, doing mindless tasks like playing computer solitaire, reading a magazine or watching an old, unexciting film or a TV repeat. Use the breathing exercises and even combine them with recorded instructions for relaxation or meditation (guided short meditations and relaxation instructions are available online).

- Avoid watching or listening to anything stimulating (like the evening news) just before bed – it's best left until next morning. Much has been written lately about avoiding exposure to *blue light* (emitted from electronic devices) during sleep. If you must have your phone or other e-devices near you, make sure that the screen light is turned away from you. If total darkness is a problem for you, a low-level night-light facing away from the bed may suffice.

- Even if late night is the only private time you have for recording your PTS notes, or reading related material, doing it then is likely to wind you up and interfere with sleep.

- Try getting up a tiny bit earlier, or finding several five-minute intervals during the day to jot down feelings and reactions.

- Before getting into bed, identify and jot down *two* things you've done during the day that you *approve* of (or are satisfied with), such as very tiny accomplishments, '*I said hello to my neighbour*', or, '*I brushed my teeth*', or a bit bigger, like '*I paid that overdue bill*'. Identifying a positive accomplishment, however small, sets the framework for a better sleep. Add to your *approval list* every night.

- It's a good idea to have a little bowl of water and a small towel beside the bed in case you awake sweating and terrified – use the dampened cloth to soothe your face and eyes and help reorientate you to the waking state. Keep a notepad and pencil beside your bed so that as soon as you wake, you can scribble down a few disturbing aspects of your dreams (and even less disturbing ones) to analyse later. If severe night sweats continue to be a problem, moisture-wicking nightshirts (in male and female sizes) are available online, sometimes from camping or mountain equipment sites, and may ease the discomfort. A small pillow covered in a comforting fabric, like suede or soft cotton, can be soothing to the touch as you settle back down to sleep.

- Although physical exercise is obviously a good

thing, don't do a workout just before bedtime – you will be too wound up to drop into a deep sleep. If you must nap during the day, jot down in your sleep diary how often that happens, and notice if it seems to help or interfere with your sleep at night.

• If you are often waking in the middle of the night, mind racing, and can't get back to sleep, it may be worth trying the **'Cognitive Shuffle'**, an original technique developed by Canadian cognitive researcher, Luc Beaudoin (2016). Because traditional sleepytime methods, like 'counting sheep', are not strong enough to counter anxious thoughts, Beaudoin suggests turning your attention to mental pictures of utterly random objects, like an egg; a boot; a fan; a lampshade; a suitcase, and so on. The chosen objects should be meaningless and not connected, like you were watching them go by in front of you on a moving sidewalk. Don't spend more than a second or two visualising each one. Eventually your brain gets 'bored' by this nonsense activity and you fall back to sleep.

• Another version of the 'Cognitive Shuffle' starts with choosing a random word, such 'hairspray', and then picturing as many (disconnected) things as you can that begin with the first letter, like, 'harbour' . . . 'handwash' . . . 'hiker'. . . etc. and then go on to the next letter, 'a' and do the same until sleep comes again. For a while, you've distracted yourself from dwelling on whatever made you anxious, which Beaudoin calls 'shuffling your thoughts to sleep' (2017). He also created an **app** called **'mySleepButton'**, which is available online.

Congratulate yourself for every small sleep gain you make.

5

Managing Your Anger

The emotional impact of post-traumatic stress will continue to ripple through your life in very intense ways. Like the tip of an iceberg, *anger*, the most noticeable emotion, will usually be found at the top. Just as powerful, but often hidden underneath, are layers of *guilt*, *grief* and *loss*, and sometimes *depression* and *despair*. Recognising these feelings, acknowledging the thoughts that are fuelling them, and working with CBT exercises to help to change your perspective can be your next challenge.

Just as you've identified *triggers* that set off your *flashbacks* and *intrusive thoughts*, the emotion of *anger* can be triggered in a split-second, by something very minor that provoked it. In an instant, you are in full 'fight or flight' mode, ready to do battle for your survival (even if the *trigger* was that someone jammed the photocopy machine or forgot to replace the top on the toothpaste!). Why are you so prone to this type of over-reaction after traumatic experiences? The answer has three parts:

- The physical arousal systems in your body.

- Your interpretation of any challenging, stressful or aggressive behaviours from others.

- The underlying feeling that your assumptions about life, the world and your safety in it have been violated and that nothing is completely safe or can be totally trusted again.

Hyper-arousal is one of the hallmark symptoms of post-traumatic stress reactions (see checklist on page 12). Highly emotional events of all types leave traces in the memory, and the catastrophic nature of your traumatic event caused biochemical changes that 'burnt' images and feelings into your memory. Some call this becoming 'hard-wired' in your arousal reactions – it takes only the slightest prodding to set off volatile behaviour. This happens because your autonomic nervous system has become 'stuck' on 'red alert' and even on a subconscious level you continue to scan for danger. Your assumptions about your personal safety in the world, along with your sense of natural justice, have been violated, and it will take concentrated effort, and time, to begin to rebuild a new protective coating on that invisible 'shield' of personal safety that helps us all to function in our everyday lives.

How can I cope when my anger reactions seem to come out in an instant?

Bring out your notebook (or e-device) and, for the next seven days, begin to track every episode of anger or outburst of irritability that you have, for example:

- **When**? Tuesday.

- **What happened?** Sarcastic comment from co-worker.

- **What I thought:** He's out to get me . . . he knows how jumpy I am and he's trying to embarrass me.

- **How I reacted:** I yelled out in the office, 'I've had enough of your sneaky comments!'

- **What I could have done differently**: I should have paused, taken a deep breath, and replied, 'No comment.'

What do you notice?

The advantage of using your notebook to keep track of your angry, irritated and frustrated feelings (even when you are keeping them to yourself and not having outbursts) is that it provides some release and even functions as a silent witness to your struggle to cope with these intense feelings. It also allows you to 'replay' the anger incident in slow motion in your mind's eye, and reflect on how you might respond differently next time you're aggravated. If possible, try not to dwell on blame or wishes for revenge, as those thoughts keep you stuck in whatever took place, wanting the other person to realise the error of his/her ways and 'play fair'.

'Justice' rarely comes in the way that you're hoping for, and you need to move forward in your thinking and realise that, in everyday, annoying interpersonal exchanges, you do always have options to interpret the situation differently and behave more appropriately – not so much for the benefit of the other person but because it keeps things *safer* for you and allows you to practise getting a better grip on your temper.

'Taking your temperature'

As you continue to work on anger management, it's helpful to look back through your notes and see if you could give each incident when you were angry, frustrated or irritated a number rating from 10 to 100. In this way you're 'taking your temperature' and beginning to pay attention to the difference in your physical and verbal reactions according to how 'hot' you rated the situation.

_____

_____

_____

'Take your temperature' activity

Try to recall and visualise your physical reactions: did your body tense up? Where were you the most tense . . . upper body . . . arms and shoulders . . . neck and face? Did your stomach go into a knot? Were you clenching your teeth? Were you sweating or getting cold? How does your body change when the situation escalates? What about tone of voice? Do you get louder as you get angrier? Now, try to picture bringing your 'temperature' down by 10 degrees at a time, starting with the 'hottest' recorded incidents . . . what do you have to do?

It's a good idea to use the '**Count to Calm**' breathing method (page 33), and you may have to talk to yourself in positive, encouraging terms if you know you have to encounter an annoying co-worker or neighbour, etc. If you always over-react to certain things, such as your teenager's messy behaviour, decide that you are going to let that go . . . just for today!

Steps in an anger management strategy for tricky interpersonal encounters

- delay (don't say anything right away)

- count (backwards, from five down to one – it serves as a distraction)

- exhale

- breathe

- talk slowly

- ask questions (get more information, rather than making accusations).

These steps allow you a few moments to cool off, and mentally take a half-step back from the situation. Repeating a 'safe word' silently to yourself (like 'chill' or 'ice cream' or 'waterslide'), will remind you to cool down quickly. Identifying a 'grounding spot' on your body, like tugging your ear lobe, or pressing the soft spot between thumb and forefinger, can also help you keep control.

Physical exercise is always a good and healthy way 'burn off steam'. If you wish, you could explore some less-traditional exercise alternatives, like yoga, t'ai chi, qigong and even salsa or dance lessons to teach you to notice how your body moves and reacts under new, positive stimulation, and to help you manage adrenaline rushes. Meditation and mindfulness training have also been exceedingly helpful to many; don't rule them out.

Caution: If you find you're taking your anger out on yourself, pulling your hair, banging your head, pounding the wall with your fist, driving dangerously or cutting yourself, it is a clear sign that your feelings are out of control and too intense to manage on your own. *Please seek the help of a professional* and remove yourself from people and situations that have the potential to trigger your urges to self-harm.

6

Coping with Guilt

One of the most pervasive emotions in the cluster of post-traumatic reactions is *guilt*. Guilt might arise from having survived in a situation when others have died (known as survivor guilt), or from having escaped or departed from a terrible geographical location when others had to stay behind (for example, journalists reporting from war-torn or disaster-ravaged countries often feel survivor guilt when they return home to peaceful surroundings to file their stories).

The thought processes behind guilt often connect with an exaggerated sense of responsibility, where you might think that, somehow, you had the 'magical' ability to have prevented the terrible thing that happened, and you failed to do so. Your thoughts are peppered with 'shoulds':

> *'I should have known!'* . . . *'I should have seen it coming!'* . . . *'I should have stopped it in time!'*

This line of thinking could be termed the 'reverse crystal ball' phenomenon. It intensifies any tendencies both to blame yourself and to criticise yourself by implying that *you* were careless and failed to prevent tragedy by not doing enough, even though in reality it would have been impossible to know what was going to happen.

It's said that the people of the Far North have dozens of words for 'snow'. This makes it possible for them to distinguish between types of snow and be better prepared for dealing with it when they go outside. Perhaps the definition of 'guilt' could be expanded in the same way, to help us realise that we often label our emotional reactions as 'guilt' when we're actually trying to describe feelings of sadness, shame, remorse, uneasiness, failed-responsibility, vengeance, unworthiness, and so on. We sometimes speak of being 'paralysed' with guilt, so it's clearly an emotion that keeps us stuck.

Shame (a close associate of guilt), is wrapped up in feeling that we don't deserve what we have: *didn't deserve to survive, don't deserve to prosper, don't deserve self-care, don't deserve to get better,* and so on. It's easy to make the connection and see how guilt and shame fit in with that third PTSD symptom cluster of *persistent negative thought/mood* shown in the Glasses of Water Illustration on page 8.

PATRICK'S STORY

Patrick was an outgoing, happily married man in his late thirties who had been driving a city bus for the past eight years. Because he often worked a late-afternoon/early-evening shift on a route that went to the outskirts of the city, he had many repeat customers who were finishing work and on their way home and he would greet everyone and often have short, pleasant exchanges. One evening, before dark, an obviously drunk man, who appeared to be living rough, staggered onto the bus and, as he attempted to pay, he was a few coins short of the fare. Instead of turning him away, Patrick, trying to keep the peace and not delay the rest of the passengers, decided to let him ride. Although the man had been given a break, as the bus started moving, he began to be belligerent with Patrick, calling him 'queer' and making racial slurs in an aggressive manner. Patrick had often been the recipient of this kind of verbal abuse while he was at school, and for a short time he 'froze' and couldn't react, just kept driving.

The passengers crouched away as the hostile man lurched further onto the bus, and finally he exited two stops later – Patrick was greatly relieved. He did not file an 'incident report' at the end of his shift, as he just wanted to get home and shake off the unsettled feelings. Unfortunately, the episode didn't end there – the next day, police notified the transit station that, the night before, a man had been apprehended for attempted robbery a short distance from that exit point, having used a knife to threaten a woman who had also left that bus. Fortunately, the woman, who was a familiar passenger to Patrick, had been able to break free and call police. She was shaken, but otherwise unharmed.

Patrick could not get the whole incident out of his mind. He went over and over it, saying to himself, *'I was just trying to help the guy out . . . I didn't realise he had a knife . . . this is all my fault . . . that woman was a friendly regular passenger, and I couldn't protect her . . . this is all my fault . . . I can't trust myself . . . I should have looked for a knife.'* Although his supervisor gave him only a mild reprimand for not writing up the incident, and told him to get on with it, Patrick felt so guilty that he suggested he be suspended (he wasn't). Despite reassurances from other drivers that 'these things happen all the time', and from his passengers that there was nothing more he could have done, Patrick was haunted by the notion that the whole incident was his fault, and that he could have prevented it. He slept very poorly and lost most of his confidence in his own judgement.

Eventually, under his supervisor's recommendation, Patrick sought counselling through his workplace assistance programme. The counsellor helped Patrick to recognise that he was holding himself 'hostage' through self-blame, even though he could not have foreseen what would happen when the passengers got off the bus.

Coping with guilt: Activity 1

Here are some of the trauma-related issues Patrick explored with his counsellor:

(You can answer the **same questions** in your notebook, as they relate to your trauma. Answer as honestly and as bluntly as you can – this is **for your eyes only!**)

- INTENTION: What was my intention in being there?

Patrick's answer: *'I was just doing my job; I tried to do the guy a good turn by letting him on; I intended to get everyone home safely.'*

- APPREHENSION: Did you have mixed emotions about it beforehand?

Patrick's answer: *'I was tired — it was late in the day . . . when he started to get on and I could smell the alcohol on him . . . I got uneasy that there might be trouble.'*

- What OUTCOME did you honestly expect?

Patrick: *'I thought I had handled things well by keeping silent through his insults. I thought he had calmed down a bit and that it was all clear when he got off the bus.'*

- How much POWER are you attributing to yourself in the situation?

Patrick: *'I have eight years of experience as a driver . . . I'm supposed to know how to handle situations like this...I expected myself to do better.'*

• Are you GUILTY for surviving and wanting your life to go on? (Yes or No) Explain.

Patrick: *'Yes! I want to forget about it and I can't . . . I just wanted that guy to disappear off my bus and I didn't care what happened to him . . . I felt relieved when he got off . . . that was careless and heartless.'*

• Are you PUNISHING yourself out of guilt? (Yes or No)

Patrick: *'Yes, I guess I am . . . I think I messed up and I don't deserve to be let off the hook . . . every time I relax for a minute, and try to feel normal, I think it's not okay to laugh a bit or to feel content.'*

Reading over your answers to the previous guilt-related questions can help you to begin to separate **facts** (what actually happened) from **feelings** (your ongoing reactions). Ask yourself if you are being overly responsible, and if you should assign at least a portion of the responsibility to others involved? Out of 100, how big a percentage would that be, for example, 50/50?, 70/30?, and so on. Are you using a judgemental double-standard, being much harder on yourself than on someone else who was part of your trauma experience? If so, treat yourself with some compassion.

Coping with guilt: Activity 2

The purpose of this activity is to help you examine your guilty thoughts and potentially reinterpret them in a balanced way. **Stop** if you become overly distressed. You can do a bit more later. Make five or six columns for your answers so that you can add material later.

Example from a traumatic situation in a sports stadium:

Two friends attended a rugby game together, a thunderstorm occurred, the crowd got unruly and one of the friends fell and hit her head, resulting in a serious concussion. The other friend was plagued by guilt.

Column 1: 'What I thought was going to happen':

'I expected that we would be at the game laughing, cheering, having snacks, feeling exhilarated and going home together.'

Pause after describing just the content of your expectations.

Column 2: Write, in shortened form, what happened:

'She was pushed by the crowd, fell and hit her head.'

Pause again after describing just the facts, as they occurred.

As you can see, this activity is attempting to help you separate your emotional reactions from the factual content of what actually happened, to assist you in becoming more objective, rather than overwhelmed by guilt.

Column 3: Is there something, however small, about which you can accept that you did the best you could? Don't deny any positive actions or belittle your efforts.

'I called for help.'

Identify any small piece of positive action that you can and **accept** it.

Column 4: What portion or 'piece' of your guilt can you let go?

'I am only responsible for half of this – the weather was responsible for some of it – the crowd was responsible too.'

Column 5: Can you now reinterpret or rename some of the emotions that may go beyond guilt into sadness or other feelings? Try to identify these.

'I feel remorseful . . . uncomfortable . . . sad . . . regretful.'

Can you put your feelings of guilt to the side now, so that they are not 'in your face' all the time? Re-read these notebook entries to help you find a better balance. Make a statement about the present, such as *'I approve of how I'm acting in this moment.'* (Activities such as meditation and mindfulness training can help you focus on the present.) Try to feel good in the here and now. Guilt is *not* a badge of dishonour. You're not 'marked'.

Sometimes traumatised people who have held religious beliefs in God or in a 'Universal Goodness' feel they have been betrayed by the spiritual forces they believed in, and then feel guilty for having these reactions. Some may feel they have been singled out for bad things to happen to them, and wrestle with guilt because they think they have brought bad luck to others. If you've been experiencing feelings of this nature, talking with a health professional or pastoral counsellor can be helpful.

If you feel an urge to make amends, make it a constructive action – do volunteer work, express appreciation to others, channel your energy in newly positive ways, do 'random acts of kindness'. You could reframe your thinking: *'My guilt is about what I can't change . . . I will allow myself to live peacefully for this moment . . . I do this to help the world.'*

7

Honouring Feelings of Grief and Loss

When someone you knew and cared about has died as part of an incident that traumatised you as well, coping with the overwhelming feelings that arise is complicated indeed. Not only are you trying to grieve for the one who was lost, you're also faced with your own losses: the loss of hopes and dreams, the interruption of future plans, the disappearance of a sense of trust and safety.

Many of the reactions that we have already discussed will be occurring at random for you: sleeplessness, surges of anger, guilt for having survived when a loved one didn't, and these may be accompanied by disbelief, a sense of helplessness, and sometimes utter despair. The post-traumatic reaction of emotional numbness may keep you going through the motions, like a robot at times, but all those suppressed feelings do not go away; they stay with you and intrude in your thoughts and behaviour.

Some grief experts suggest that you need to work on and at least partially resolve your own traumatic experience before you can effectively grieve the loss of another. Unfortunately, society expects us to do the opposite – bury the dead, reconcile the loss, be grateful that you survived, and, within about six weeks, 'move on with your life'! This type of social pressure from well-meaning individuals is unrealistic and often increases feelings of isolation while you're still grieving.

Grief has a public face and a private face. Reactions and timetables are individual – up to you! Because so many terrible incidents occur now that involve death and injury on a large scale, there is pressure to begin memorials immediately, while people are still in shock, and for those involved, even indirectly, to participate in public events and give interviews or comments to the press.

If you've been involved in a large-scale terrible incident, whether a fire, mass evacuation, murder in your neighbourhood, or you were a witness to violence that was traumatising for *you*, it might feel like you're less worthy of attention if you weren't visibly injured while others were. It's important that you have a place where you can tell all aspects of *your* story, say how it *affects you,* and give your testimony, privately, as posting too much personal commentary online on social media sites sometimes invites unwanted criticism when you were seeking support. Time to get out your notebook!

Activity 1: Your untold story

Your notebook can become sort of a 'safety deposit box' that can hold your unspoken thoughts and feelings of grief and loss. After participating in the formal, expected grief rituals, such as funerals and memorials, you're likely to have 'unfinished business' that's difficult or inappropriate to talk through with those around you. Sometimes it's about someone you loved briefly or weren't supposed to have loved, a departed pet, a baby given up for adoption years before, or angry feelings that were never resolved between you and a family member or ex-spouse.

Put down in detail things you've never told anyone – sights, sounds, touch sensations, conversations that you recall. Don't censor your expressions – let it all come out on paper. You may end up facing events from the past that have been blocked out for a long time. This can be a lonely activity, but it's an opportunity to face your own feelings, go over what you wish you'd said, and how you wanted the other (now lost) person to respond. Try to identify and write about the *'worst part'*, that little terrible detail that is sticking with you and that makes it so hard to imagine getting on with your life.

Traumatic grief can change your sense of your own identity. Losing a skill or ability, a good job, even loss of a caregiving role can leave you feeling *empty* and confused. Look through your notes with a CBT viewpoint – are you using 'all or nothing' thinking to judge yourself? Are you predicting the future in 'always or never' terms? Are you labelling yourself as a 'failure' or a 'disappointment' to others? These are all exaggerated thinking styles that perpetuate the negative and feed depressed feelings. Start to make peace with yourself by writing small, encouraging statements. A more gentle approach includes identifying one small thing at a time that you've done *right*, and gradually adding to that list.

You might be angry because close friends have stopped coming around to support you and treat you like everything is 'fine'. 'Talk back' to them in your notebook before you have face-to-face confrontations. Are you expecting others to read your mind and know what you need, even though you avoid telling them?

A special journal, or a separate file or section in your notebook, will be a place to write letters and have an outlet as you go on. Talking out loud to the departed can help – if you don't have a private place to do that, *thinking* through those conversations 'out loud' to yourself works, too.

Activity 2: Write a letter and 'send' it

Even if you've participated in public memorials, it can help to design your own personal goodbye ritual, or private memorial. For example, you may want to **write a letter** to a departed loved one (even if that was an unborn child, or a stillbirth, or even one of your own limbs that was amputated), saying how much you cared, how much you miss them, describing how deep are your feelings of loss. Just as happened when you were writing your *untold story* in your notebook, likely tears and pent-up emotions will be released with this activity. You can 'send' the letter by storing it in a private place, burying it, or burning it and scattering the ashes.

No one wants to be grieving – they want it to be over, but they want the thing/person they have lost back too – they're caught in a circle of needing to accept what is lost and not being able to realise that it's really gone.

Coping with troubling recollections

Troubling recurrent images of a dead one can be dealt with using an imaginary *'split screen'*, where on one side you visualise your loved one peacefully sleeping or smiling happily, and on the other side is the death or injury image that haunts your imagination. Gradually 'dim down' the troubling image, as you brighten up the comforting one. That's how you want to remember – what they looked like in their life, not in their death.

Grieving physical losses

When the loss involves permanent or semi-permanent changes in physical abilities, facial disfigurement or sensory impairment, most find it difficult to carry on and accept what has happened. Feeling that your body has betrayed you or that fate has betrayed you and questioning whether you want to live with your changed appearance or weakened abilities are normal first reactions. Rehabilitation of your emotional well-being is as vitally important as meeting the physical challenges of recovery. Do not suffer on your own – seek psychological support and accept help if it's available. Your task is to reclaim your body as it is now and regain a sense of control and purpose.

Activity 3: Columns in your notebook

When you feel able, use your notebook to make two lists: **'*Things I miss*'** and **'*Things I don't miss*'**. These lists might be about a departed one, or about aspects of your life before that are gone now. The purpose is to help you become a little bit objective, and face your feelings a bit at a time. The hardest part for many, and the stage where we often

---

get stuck in grieving, is feeling that we are being disloyal to a loved one if we relax for a few moments, and enjoy something pleasant, without thinking of the one we have lost. We're afraid to forget or to seem as if we've moved beyond our grief and thus portray that our loss was not so important. Sometimes feelings about what has been lost are mixed or ambivalent – there may be relief that the person didn't live to suffer, even though they're truly missed. Try to pinpoint, in your notebook, what is getting in the way of your healing and of resolving your loss.

Much has been written about stages of grief, which implies that grief proceeds in an orderly fashion, from 'shock' to 'resolution'. Unfortunately, the grief process is a messy emotional roller-coaster that might take you through all the stages in one day or one week, and then be back to start at the following week. During the first year, every three or four months, distressing feelings are likely to shift, and often come back forcefully, but the length of time you're in intense distress subsides more quickly.

Working through grief

It may take a long time to reach the 'acceptance' stage, but by recognising and working through your emotional reactions, you can move grief/loss images alongside of you, rather than seeing them in front of your face all the time.

Put off impulsive decisions, like selling the house, quitting your job, and so on for eight months to a year, unless you are in an unsafe situation, or have to do so out of financial necessity. These spur-of-the-moment actions can seem like a way to avoid or distract yourself from the pain of the loss, but you are not likely to be ready to anticipate all the consequences fully.

You might explore online to find specific grief groups (such as 'young widows' or 'traumatised bystanders') or inquire at local community centres. Connecting with others in similar situations can be reassuring and reduce your sense of isolation.

Anniversary reactions

Anniversary reactions are surprisingly common and may take you by surprise if you feel you've been quite resolved about your traumatic experience. Even years later, things may be going along well, and then, suddenly, you're irritable, sleeping poorly, agitated and upset without knowing why. Ask yourself if you're coming close to an anniversary of the trauma, and, if so, your symptoms may make sense and you can expect them to diminish once the actual anniversary date has passed. It seems like your body/mind subconsciously keeps its own 'calendar' of the traumatic event and reminds you that the date is coming.

Planning ahead of time for the whole day of a trauma anniversary, even if you don't stick to your first plan, keeps you from being taken by surprise by your reactions. You might have breakfast by candlelight, buy flowers for yourself, play special music, sit in a park for a while, volunteer or donate to a shelter in their honour, or revisit the scene if you wish. Any slight change in routine to mark the day can serve as a reminder to be gentle with yourself on this emotional anniversary.

8

Overcoming Avoidance Behaviours, Emotional Numbness and Harmful Urges

As discussed earlier, avoidance reactions form a large cluster of the core symptoms of PTSD. The notion that if we *stop thinking about it, refuse to talk about it, and, especially, don't allow ourselves to feel it, all will be well*, is misguided at best, and detrimental to recovery at worst. Unfortunately, the more we try to avoid triggering memories of trauma (either consciously or unconsciously) by limiting interactions and suppressing feelings, the greater the distance we are creating between ourselves and those around us, particularly those we have intimate connections with.

Putting on a brave face and avoiding the true emotions simmering under the surface makes coming to terms with things more difficult over time. Trying to avoid or suppress emotions opens the pathway to substance abuse and increased isolation, from yourself and from your loved ones. Blocked emotional responses can build up and then flood out inappropriately in anger or self-abusive behaviour, pushing others further away.

Being unable to express loving feelings and respond to others in the way you normally did before your trauma can leave you feeling like a stranger in your own skin. Nothing feels and looks like it did before – you're 'set apart' and may even have brief anxious episodes when you feel like you're outside your own body, watching everyone but separated from them, like being behind a glass wall.

With the numbing of your emotional responses, you tend to be caught up in your own world, not because you are intentionally shutting others out, but rather, you're preoccupied with the aftermath of your trauma and your usual ways of interacting have been shattered.

Family members may be patient with you for a fairly long time, but after a while, as they watch you staring into space, or looking blank when asked a question about everyday matters, irritation may set in, and they might accuse you of *'not being with it'*, or being *'totally self-absorbed'*. These comments from loved ones might seem to imply that 'a stronger person could cope better with this', and can cause deep blows to your sense of confidence, resulting in lower self-worth. Your thoughts may be full of self-recriminations and self-doubts: '*I'm going crazy and that's why I can't cope . . . I can't count on myself to react appropriately anymore!*'

Your thick wall of emotional scar tissue may keep you feeling like an imposter; for example, you go through the motions, but you continue to believe that, if your loved ones really knew what was going on inside you, they could never accept the 'real' you as you are now. Remember, all of this is commonly felt as part of post-traumatic stress reactions, and therefore, feelings are *not* truth! Keep reminding yourself of that.

DEREK'S STORY

It all started with a hospital visit . . . although I had a chronic condition for many years, it was well-managed with medication and regular medical check-ups. Unexpectedly, I developed a blockage and found myself in the emergency ward, facing immediate surgery. Complications developed, and I ended up with multiple subsequent surgeries, and a temporary 'appliance', which made me feel like my body didn't belong to me anymore. I spent weeks in the intensive care unit, where heavy-duty pain medication and being on a ventilator made me lose all sense of time and have delusions of monsters and strange experiences. As I hovered between life and death, I couldn't communicate with my loved ones who stood by horrified.

It took me over a year to even *begin* the emotional recovery. Flashbacks and nightmares continued for months, and I'd lost chunks of memory of what happened, and couldn't trust the distorted recall I did have. I felt totally vulnerable and deeply depressed. I also felt guilty that my loved ones had to go through this with me – why me?

Now my medical check-ups re-trigger many horror feelings, and I avoid visiting anyone in hospital, even when I should be going to see them. It's so *isolating* because no one can understand what I've been through. I appear physically fine now, and well-meaning people minimise the whole experience, saying, 'You must be so happy now that you came through this so well!' That's not how I feel, but I can't say so.

I can't talk to my partner because we're both traumatised, and don't remember things the same way. She had to watch me almost die and be revived eight times, and now she wants to talk about how hard that was for her . . . I can't help her, and I can't discuss it.

It helped me to know that this was post-traumatic stress; I began to understand that my symptoms and reactions were reasonable, and that I was not going insane. My whole concept of safety and confidence in dealing with life is *gone*, and it's a hard road to get it back. I'm trying to re-establish my faith in life in small ways.

While a 'ripple effect' of PTS reactions can cause relationships to break down as loved ones and friends lose patience with you, you can avoid worsening the situation by reflecting on your current thoughts and behaviours and recognising whether you're not allowing yourself to be loved again. Maybe you are avoiding intimacy for fear of rejection, or because you think you would be overwhelmed by intense emotion?

Instead of feeling trapped by emotion, start to deal with it: face your fears of closeness and commit a certain small amount of time each day (even five minutes) to recording your feelings in your notebook. Just as you have done in earlier CBT exercises, you can identify *triggers* that are spurring you to avoid closeness/intimacy, perhaps for fear that you'll 'contaminate' your partner if you reveal the horror of your traumatic memories. You may be wary of joining closely with another in case the few protective defences you have left will break down.

As you begin, set very small, achievable goals (like touching your partner gently on the arm and saying '*I'm glad you're here*'). Accept the pain of dealing with these reconnection attempts but give it time limits and boundaries. Stop pretending. Don't do the impossible; the 'small and possible' will move things forward.

Compassion for yourself is essential for healing. Any plan to expose yourself gradually to places, things or people that you've been avoiding since the trauma should be approached cautiously and gently, and, if possible, with the guidance and support of a trained professional.

Resisting harmful urges

Urges for escape, blotting out the pain of your traumatic memories, and ending it all come from very dark places of mind and thought. Trying to 'get away from it all' can take extreme forms, such as overuse and abuse of alcohol and drugs, gambling (including over-buying of lottery tickets), self-harm (head banging, cutting, pounding the wall with your fist, sugar-bingeing), high-speed reckless driving, crossing carelessly in traffic, going alone to areas at night where you are likely to be in harm's way, or visiting places where you could be tempted to throw yourself over a cliff or swim in dangerous currents. Such desperate attempts to 'roll the dice', letting *chance* decide if you live or die, are based on misguided thinking that everyone (including yourself) would be better off if you weren't here. Anxiety may be reduced 'in the moment' by these behaviours, but this relief is short-lived.

The impulse to commit suicide is pain-driven, and the urges are strongest when the sufferer is sleep-deprived. Any action you can take to establish *safety*, even temporarily (for yourself or for someone else who is wrestling with suicidal impulses), can delay the impulse for destructive behaviour and open the door for other factors to be considered. Substituting one 'tolerable' form of pain for the buried, deeper emotional pain is not the answer. Postponing a suicide decision, even one day at a time, and getting some sleep can allow your thinking to take a different turn.

Catastrophic events, like your traumatic experience, occur at random, *not* 'for a reason', and *not* 'because you deserved it'. Look for new reason and meaning that will help you to move forward – caring for an animal, helping out at a shelter, performing a random act of kindness. Don't hesitate to ask for help by contacting a help centre or calling a crisis line, or getting in touch with an old friend. The unwelcome, destructive feelings can become less urgent if you are able to recognise some value in yourself.

9

Looking Ahead – Going Further

Therapy Options and Support Networks

What can I expect from the future? How can I put this all behind me?

This book has provided you with an overview of the issues and symptoms that arise with post-traumatic stress reactions. The exercises and strategies to help you manage your PTS responses are based on cognitive behavioural therapy, a widely recommended treatment style. Some people, especially those who have had a *single* traumatic event, may benefit greatly from the type of self-help approach outlined here, and may even find it sufficient to help them resolve their difficulties. Others, especially those who have experienced ongoing and very complex traumatic situations (such as prolonged abuse, combat exposure or hostage-takings), may find beginning steps here, and the material may help to sustain them while they are working with family doctors or health centres and awaiting referrals to more specific trauma therapy services.

For more detailed presentations of guided self-help material, the following resources are **strongly recommended**. Both are written by leading consultant clinical psychologists who head PTSD treatment centres.

- *Overcoming Traumatic Stress*, 2nd **Ed. by Claudia Herbert**, Robinson, 2017.

  A self-help guide using cognitive behavioural techniques. This revised and expanded version of the 2008 edition of *Overcoming Traumatic Stress* (co-authored by Claudia Herbert and Ann Wetmore), features state-of-the-art cognitive exercises, new PTS coping strategies, in-depth discussions and helpful chapter summaries.

- *The Compassionate Mind Approach to Recovering from Trauma* **by Deborah A. Lee & Sophie James**, Robinson, 2012 (available in North America as *The Compassionate Guide to Recovering from Trauma and PTSD* [New Harbinger, 2011]).

> Self-directed treatment guide using innovative and restorative compassion-focused therapy (CFT) techniques (pioneered by the author) as a means to overcome flashbacks, shame, guilt and fear, and move towards healing.

Will I ever be rid of these reactions?

Even when PTS reactions seem quite resolved, they can be re-triggered by large-scale catastrophes, such as natural and man-made disasters, acts of terrorism, and some of the 'weather horror' that has recently given rise to mass destruction through floods, wildfires, snow and windstorms, explosions, etc. These occurrences seem to betray the natural order of the global climate and may leave you feeling unsafe again. Group support after such events can be helpful in keeping you connected with others and not isolated. Take up whatever public help/therapeutic support is on offer immediately following such incidents – making sure you are 'counted' at the outset of a large-scale traumatic event gives you access to whatever benefits and supports for survivors and families that are arranged later, and you can *choose* which ones are most appropriate for you as time goes on.

Beyond self-help: considering a therapist

When it's evident to you, to your healthcare provider, and/or to those closest to you, that your personal struggles with post-traumatic issues are getting the best of you, and your present coping strategies are not sufficient, it's a good idea to start with your doctor, district nurse, or community health centre to discuss what options are available and what further treatments and other resources may be right for you.

Therapy options:

While there are many different therapy/counselling approaches, it's important that your therapist has training related to PTSD and is able to incorporate a trauma-focused approach into your sessions.

- **Trauma-Focused Cognitive Behavioural Therapy** (TF-CBT) is generally a short or moderate-term intervention (eight to twenty sessions) sensitive to the emotional needs of youth, adult survivors and families struggling with specific after-effects of traumatic experiences. Cognitive techniques are aimed at modifying distorted thinking and reducing negative reactions, while building confidence and stress management.

The most widely researched and evidence-based therapies for PTSD include: Cognitive Processing Therapy (CPT), Prolonged Exposure therapy (PE), and Eye Movement Desensitisation and Reprocessing (EMDR).

- **Cognitive Processing Therapy** teaches clients how to recognise the negative 'stuck points' in their world view that resulted from their trauma, often through writing and reviewing a detailed, private, full description of their traumatic event. The aim is to work through the feelings arising now and achieve a more balanced and emotionally manageable viewpoint.

- **Prolonged Exposure Therapy** has been very effective in systematically reducing the intense fear responses stemming from recall of the 'worst parts' of traumatic memories, and thus making it possible for clients to participate in previously-avoided, safe activities that have unfortunately become triggers for PTS reactions. In weekly or bi-weekly sessions, clients are taught a relaxation/controlled breathing exercise and encouraged to describe aloud, in vivid detail, their traumatic experience(s). Repeated listening to their recordings of memories that had been strenuously avoided, both in-session, and later at home, while practising the managed breathing/relaxation techniques allows clients to gradually de-condition debilitating fear and avoidance reactions.

- **Eye Movement Desensitisation and Reprocessing** is generally a brief intervention based on the idea that the traumatic memory is stored as 'raw data' along with any misconceptions or distorted thinking that occurred at the same moments in time. In order to allow this emotional material to be 'reprocessed', the client is asked to bring to mind a vivid picture of the traumatic encounter, along with a distorted belief, such as, 'I should have been able to stop it; I'm useless'. While doing the imaginary paired recall, the client is instructed to follow the clinician's finger with their eyes, from left to right, repeating several times. If other traumatic images emerge, the cycle is repeated. Later, the client practises linking a more desired thought, such as, 'I can trust myself to cope in a crisis situation', with remaining images of trauma(s), thus increasing a sense of mastery.

New and alternative PTSD support options

The global 'Mindfulness Movement' has been integrated into a number of therapeutic pursuits, and the practice of mindfulness, which includes a present-centred, meditative approach to interacting with the world, has helped many, including PTSD sufferers, to feel grounded in the present moment, with less anxiety and a reduced sense of being over-whelmed. Mindfulness training is available in many community centres, and many simple meditative exercises are available online.

- A quick mindfulness practice is called '*Noticing*', which involves using your five senses to focus your attention in the present moment: 'What do you *see* in front of you?'; 'What do you *hear* beside you?'; 'What does the air you are breathing in *smell* like?'; 'What is the taste lingering on your lips?'; 'How does it feel when you place your hand over your heart with a gentle *touch*?'.

- **Acceptance and Commitment Therapy** (ACT) uses acceptance and mindfulness strategies to help individuals achieve 'psychological flexibility', that is, instead of over-reacting or attempting to avoid or suppress distressing feelings, clients are encouraged to notice, accept, and move on, while building on small behavioural changes that reflect the values and meaning of their core selves. ACT has been effective for many in helping them to manage chronic pain and connect with the value of life in the present.

Beyond therapy or guided self-help, many people living with PTSD have found support, comfort and improved coping ability through the use of *specially trained 'therapy' animals (usually dogs)*, who can sense when their owners are becoming tense, anxious and symptomatic in situations, and signal them to take calming actions, such as relaxed breathing. While there may be a long waiting list for formally certified service dogs, or the expense may be prohibitive, other interactive encounters, such as volunteering at an animal rescue shelter or dog-training programme can also be beneficial.

Practices that involve tending or caring for animals (or plants) can restore a sense of identity and personal effectiveness. Some equestrian centres offer day programmes of *'therapy' with horses*. Many report that learning to relate to such large animals with patience and new-found skill is 'life-changing'.

Training in *meditation* and the soft martial arts, such as *tai chi, yoga, qi gong* etc., can improve overall health and well-being as well as providing psychological strengthening. Becoming more grounded and less reactive, especially in trigger situations, reduces anxiety and promotes calming self-management.

One of the more surprising adaptations of trauma support programmes has occurred in the teaching of *glass-blowing* to those with PTSD. Because strong traumatic reactions often rob individuals of the ability to live in the present moment, this beautiful, highly skilled and somewhat dangerous artistic endeavour rebuilds cognitive skills by requiring those who undertake it to focus, concentrate, and balance risk with the opportunity to create.

Another innovation has been the publication of adult 'comics' – computer-generated graphic illustrations of traumatic events, PTSD reactions and survival stories aimed at PTSD sufferers and their families. Easy to read and relate to, they promote discussion on all levels, reduce stigma, and make reoccurring symptoms easier to understand for all.

Two great examples of PTSD comics are:

- *The Enemy Within*, #1 in the 'Stranger Returns' series, by Belinda M. Seagram & Martin R. Crawford (2017). **www.ptsdherocomics.com**

- *Trauma is Really Strange*, by Steve Haines, art by Sophie Standing (2016). This small volume illustrates and explains the effects of trauma on your brain and physiology. www.stevehaines.net. **www.traumaisreallystrange.com**

New 'apps' for electronic devices are appearing frequently and can be very helpful in reducing anxiety and providing on-the-spot coaching for those with PTSD.

10

Recommended Resources and References

Highly recommended:
(see chapter 9 for descriptions)

Overcoming Traumatic Stress, 2nd Ed. by Claudia Herbert, Robinson, 2017.

The Compassionate Mind Approach to Recovering from Trauma by Deborah A. Lee and Sophie James, Robinson, 2012 (available in North America as *The Compassionate Guide to Recovering from Trauma and PTSD* [New Harbinger, 2011]).

Other useful books:

Get Out of Your Mind and Into Your Life: The New Acceptance & Commitment Therapy by Steven C. Hayes with Spencer Smith, New Harbinger, 2005.

Mind-Body Workbook for PTSD: a 10-week Program for Healing After Trauma by Stanley H. Block and Carolyn Bryant Block, New Harbinger, 2010.

Feeling Good: The New Mood Therapy by David D. Burns, Avon Books, 2009 – revised and updated.

Good Grief Rituals: Tools for Healing by E. Childs-Gowell, Station Hill Press, 1995.

Trust After Trauma: A Guide to Relationships for Survivors and Those Who Love Them by Aphrodite Matsakis, New Harbinger, 1998.

Many titles in the **Overcoming** series, and the **Introduction to Coping** series, are now available in revised editions, published by Robinson. Specially recommended are:

Overcoming Grief and *An Introduction to Coping with Grief* by Sue Morris.

Overcoming Anxiety by Helen Kennerley and *An Introduction to Coping with Anxiety* by Brenda Hogan and Lee Brosan.

Overcoming Depression by Paul Gilbert and *An Introduction to Coping with Depression* by Lee Brosan and Brenda Hogan.

Useful websites:

United Kingdom:

UK Psychological Trauma Society (UKPTS) – lists trauma services in the UK.

www.ukpts.co.uk

PTSD UK – a charity that raises awareness and publishes a list of trauma treatment providers through private or NHS services.

www.ptsduk.org

The Oxford Development Centre – a centre for Trauma Healing and Growth. A long-established private specialist trauma therapy service (since 1997).

www.oxdev.co.uk

The British Psychological Society.

www.bps.org.uk

British Association for Counselling & Psychotherapy (BACP).

www.bacp.co.uk

USA:

American Psychological Association – PTSD

**www.apa.org/about/offices/directorates/
guidelines/ptsd.pdf**

National Center for PTSD – VA Mental Health Crisis Resources for Veterans, Families and Friends, including children with PTSD Parent.

**www.ptsd.va.gov/public/family/re
sources_family_friends.asp**

International Society for Traumatic Stress Studies (ISTSS) Find-a-Clinician Service for USA, Canada, and International, Assessment and Resource Materials.

www.istss.org

CANADA:

Canadian Psychological Association – Traumatic Stress Section.

**www.cpa.ca/aboutcpa.cpasections/
traumaticstress/**

TEMA.CA

'Canada's Leading Provider of Peer Support, Family Assistance, etc. for Public Safety & Military

Personnel Dealing with Mental Health Injuries.'
Resources and crisis centres are listed by
Province. US addiction/rehab. centres included.

www.tema.ca/resource-links

Canadian Resource Centre for Victims of Crime
– Canadian Resources for Treatment of Post-
Traumatic Stress Disorder. Resources listed by
Province, including health and social service
centres, and private practitioners with rates.

www.trauma-ptsd.com/en/ressources

MOBILE APP:

PTSD COACH CANADA – Mobile Application

Innovative resource from Veterans Affairs Canada
available for all e-devices 'to help learn about and
manage symptoms that occur after trauma.'

**www.veterans.gc.ca/eng/stay-connected/
mobile-app/ptsd-coach-canada**

NOVA SCOTIA:

Association of Psychologists of Nova Scotia – Keeps
referral listing of private practitioners by area,
including trauma service providers.

www.apns.ca

Landing Strong. PTSD treatment centre in Windsor, N.S. established 2018 by Dr. Belinda Seagram, Clinical Psychologist – provides on-site services, and weekly e-newsletter re PTSD issues; publishes PTSDherocomics.com.

www.LandingStrong.com

Rally Point Retreat, Sable River, N.S. Respite facility open to anyone diagnosed with PTSD and under care, providing a non-treatment 'safe' space, newly established by Bob and Johan Grundy (2018).

www.rallypointretreat.org

REFERENCES

American Psychiatric Association (APA – 2013). *Diagnostic and Statistical Manual of Mental Disorders* (5th ed.; DSM-5). Washington, D.C.:APA.

Beck, Aaron T., Rush, A. John, Shaw, Brian F., & Emery, Gary. *Cognitive Therapy of Depression*. The Guildford Press, 1987.

Beaudoin, Luc (2016, 2017). British Columbia cognitive research scientist who developed the 'Cognitive Shuffle' technique for reducing insomnia, as discussed by Oliver Burkeman in *The Guardian*, Life and Style section, 15 July 2016.

'Shuffle' quote taken from CBC News interview, posted online 30 April 2017.

www.cbc.ca/news/canada/british-colum bia/sfu-sleep-trick-luc-beaudoin-1.4092294

Lancaster, C.L., Teeters, J.B., Gros, D.F., & Sudie, E. Back. 'Posttraumatic Stress Disorder: Overview of Evidence-Based Assessment and Treatment.' *Journal of Clinical Medicine* 2016 Nov. 5(11): 105. Published online 22 November 2016.

An Introduction to Coping with Insomnia and Sleep Problems

2nd Edition

Colin A. Espie

Available to buy in ebook and paperback

An invaluable guide to sleep problems from a leading expert

Poor sleep can have a huge impact on our health and wellbeing, leaving us feeling run-down, exhausted and stressed out. This self-help guide explains the causes of insomnia and why it is so difficult to break bad habits. This updated edition gives you clinically proven cognitive behavioural therapy (CBT) techniques for improving the quality of your sleep:

Keeping a sleep diary

Setting personal goals

Improving your sleep hygiene

Dealing with a racing mind

Making lasting improvements to your sleeping and waking pattern

An Introduction to Coping with Phobias

2nd Edition

Brenda Hogan

Available to buy in ebook and paperback

Learn how to overcome your phobias

It is very common for people to have a phobia of something – heights, spiders, water. . . but when that fear prevents you from doing the things you enjoy in life, or causes you deep anxiety and feelings of panic, it is time to seek help.

This self-help guide explains how phobias develop and what keeps them going. This updated edition gives you clinically proven cognitive behavioural therapy (CBT) techniques to help you challenge the way you think and behave in order to treat your phobias:

Set goals and start to face your fears

Avoid relapses and learn to problem-solve

An Introduction to Coping with Health Anxiety

2nd Edition

Brenda Hogan and Charles Young

Available to buy in ebook and paperback

Learn how to control your health anxiety

Health anxiety affects many people across the world – a preoccupation with physical illness that is equally bad for your mental health. This self-help guide explains how it develops and what keeps it going. This updated edition gives you clinically proven cognitive behavioural therapy (CBT) techniques to help you challenge the way you think and behave:

Spot and challenge thoughts that make you anxious

Reduce your focus on your body and on illness

An Introduction to Coping with Panic

2nd Edition

Charles Young

Available to buy in ebook and paperback

Learn how to manage your feelings of panic

Panic disorder and panic attacks affect many people across the world. This self-help guide explains what panic attacks are, how panic develops and what keeps it going.

This updated edition gives you clinically proven cognitive behavioural therapy (CBT) techniques to help you recognise the link between your thoughts and your panic:

Spot and challenge thoughts that make you panic

Keep a panic diary

Learn calming breathing techniques

An Introduction to Coping with Stress

2nd Edition

Lee Brosan

Available to buy in ebook and paperback

Practical support for how to overcome stress

We all know what stress feels like, and indeed what it feels like when we have too much stress in our lives. Too much stress can have a negative impact on us, almost without our noticing it. It can affect our family life, friendships and other relationships, our work life and our physical and emotional wellbeing.

Written by an experienced practitioner and author of the popular self-help title *Overcoming Stress*, this introductory book can help you if stress has become a problem, using cognitive behavioural therapy (CBT) strategies to:

Help you recognise what happens when you are under stress

Change how you feel, think and act in order to regain
a more balanced outlook

Manage everyday life more effectively

An Introduction to Coping with Grief

2nd Edition

Sue Morris

Available to buy in ebook and paperback

Learn how to cope following the death of a loved one

Grief is a natural reaction to loss but in some cases it can be devastating, preventing you from moving on in your life and affecting your relationships and work. This fully updated self-help guide offers an examination and explanation of the grieving process and outlines clinically-proven strategies, based on cognitive behavioural therapy (CBT), to help you adjust to life without a loved one:

Knowing what to expect when you are grieving

Understanding the physical and psychological
reactions to grief

Practical coping strategies to help you deal with your loss

An Introduction to Coping with Extreme Emotions:

A Guide to Borderline or Emotionally Unstable Personality Disorder

Lee Brosan and Amanda Spong

Available to buy in ebook and paperback

Learn how to cope with extreme or unstable emotions

Many people suffer from extreme emotions with around 2% of people being diagnosed with Borderline Personality Disorder. It is a very troubling condition which causes abnormal and unstable behaviour including overwhelming feelings of distress and anger, which may lead to self-harming, damage or destruction of relationships and, at times, loss of contact with reality.

Through clinically proven dialectical behaviour therapy (DBT) techniques, this book will help you to control your extreme emotions. You will learn:

The symptoms of personality disorder

Different ways of coping with overwhelming emotions

How to increase your emotional resilience from day to day

An Introduction to Coping with Depression

2nd Edition

Lee Brosan and Brenda Hogan

Available to buy in ebook and paperback

Practical support for how to overcome depression and low mood

Depression is the predominant mental health condition worldwide, affecting millions of people each year. But it can be treated effectively with cognitive behavioural therapy (CBT).

Written by experienced practitioners, this introductory book explains what depression is and how it makes you feel. It will help you to understand your symptoms and is ideal as an immediate coping strategy and as a preliminary to fuller therapy. You will learn:

How depression develops and what keeps it going

How to spot and challenge thoughts that maintain your depression

Problem solving and balanced thinking skills

Introduction to Coping with Obsessive Compulsive Disorder

2nd Edition

Lee Brosan

Available to buy in ebook and paperback

Practical support for how to overcome obsessive compulsive disorder

Obsessive compulsive disorder (OCD) affects millions of people each year. But it can be treated effectively with cognitive behavioural therapy (CBT).

Written by an experienced practitioner, this introductory book explains what OCD is, what different forms it takes and how it can make you feel. It will help you to understand your symptoms and is ideal as an immediate coping strategy and as a preliminary to fuller therapy. You will learn:

How OCD develops and what keeps it going

The role that intrusive thoughts play in your compulsive behaviour

Cognitive skills and exposure and response prevention techniques